Backyard Animals
Eagles

Edited by Heather C. Hudak

Weigl Publishers Inc.

Published by Weigl Publishers Inc.
350 5th Avenue, Suite 3304, PMB 6G
New York, NY 10118-0069
Website: www.weigl.com

Library of Congress Cataloging-in-Publication Data available upon request.
Fax 1-866-44-WEIGL for the attention of the Publishing Records department.

ISBN 978-1-60596-002-9 (hard cover)
ISBN 978-1-60596-008-1 (soft cover)

Printed in the United States of America
1 2 3 4 5 6 7 8 9 0 12 11 10 09 08

Editor Heather C. Hudak
Design Terry Paulhus

All of the Internet URLs given in the book were valid at the time of publication.
However, due to the dynamic nature of the Internet, some addresses may have
changed, or sites may have ceased to exist since publication. While the author
and publisher regret any inconvenience this may cause readers, no responsibility
for any such changes can be accepted by either the author or the publisher.

Photo Credits

Weigl acknowledges Getty Images as its primary image supplier for this title.

Every reasonable effort has been made to trace ownership and to obtain
permission to reprint copyright material. The publishers would be pleased
to have any errors or omissions brought to their attention so that they may
be corrected in subsequent printings.

Contents

Meet the Eagle

Eagles are birds of prey. These birds hunt other animals for food. Eagles are warm-blooded animals that lay eggs. They have feathers, a beak with no teeth, and a small skeleton.

Eagles are different from other birds of prey, such as owls and hawks. They are larger, heavier, and more powerful. Their hooked beaks, strong legs, and powerful **talons** make it easy for them to prey on other animals. Sharp eyesight helps them spot their prey from high above.

Eagles live in every kind of **habitat**, including forests, wetlands, deserts, mountains, and farmlands. They can also live in towns and cities with parks.

An eagle's feathers, beak, and talons are made of keratin. Human fingernails are made of the same substance.

Eagles have hollow bones that are lightweight. This helps the birds to fly.

All about Eagles

Eagles come from a family of birds called *Accipitridae*. This family includes many other birds of prey, such as hawks and kites. Eagles are divided into four groups based on how they look and behave.

Fish and snake eagles get their names from their diet of fish and snakes. Those that live in the tropical rain forests are called forest eagles. Booted eagles get their name from their feathered feet, which look like boots.

Eagles can be many sizes. Booted eagles are known to be the smallest eagles. They weigh just over 2 pounds (1 kilogram). The largest eagles in the world are the giant forest eagles. They weigh about 20 pounds (9 kg).

The bald eagle was declared the national bird of the United States in 1782.

Where Eagles Live

Fish Eagle

- Found in Africa, Europe, and North America

Snake Eagle

- Found in Africa, India, and the Middle East

Booted or True Eagle

- Found in Asia, Europe, and North Africa

Giant Forest Eagle

- Found in tropical rain forests around the world

Eagle History

Birds developed 250 million years ago when *pterodactyls*, or flying dinosaurs, developed into birds. Dinosaurs are thought to be the bird's closest relatives. They share similar bony features and behavior.

As the weather on Earth started to change, dinosaurs died. Birds were able to survive the changes because of their ability to fly.

Early humans used to train eagles to help them hunt animals. Today, this sport is known as falconry.

Fascinating Facts

Fossil remains of ancient eagles date back about 25 million years, long before humans lived on Earth.

Eagles are usually brown, black, or gray in color to blend in with the environment.

Eagle Habitat

Eagles are found all over the world. The bald eagle and the golden eagle are some of the most common eagles in North America.

Eagles live in forests, mountains, and deserts. Bald eagles live near water bodies such as lakes and rivers. Eagles **migrate** south in winter in search of warmer climates and food supplies.

A male and a female eagle build a nest together. It is called an eyrie and is found in tall trees or on high cliffs. The nests are made of sticks and are lined with twigs, grass, and feathers. Eagles use the same nest every year, mending it every spring.

Some eagle nests may reach 10 feet (30 meters) across and weigh as much as 2,000 pounds (900 kg).

Black-chested snake eagles live in the deserts of Africa and feed on snakes and lizards.

Eagle Features

Eagle bodies are made for flying and catching prey. They have many features that help them do these tasks. For example, eagles' feathers keep the birds warm and waterproof.

EYES
Eagles have bright yellow eyes. Their sharp vision helps them spot their prey from a great distance. They can see clearly during the day, but not at night.

BEAK
Eagles have a large, hooked beak. It is powerful and can easily tear the flesh of prey. Eagles have no teeth.

WINGS
Eagles have strong, broad wings, so they can fly high without much effort. On average, they can fly at a speed of 31 miles (50 kilometers) per hour.

LEGS
Eagles have two legs, with short, powerful toes, and long talons. The sharp talons pierce the prey and help hold it firmly in place.

What Do Eagles Eat?

Eagles are **carnivores**. They mostly eat meat such as rabbits, turtles, and ducks. At times, eagles steal food from other eagles.

Eagles swoop down from the sky to grab prey with their strong talons. The talons are razor-sharp and curved to hold prey. Eagles eat by holding prey in one claw and tearing the flesh with the other.

Eagles can swim to the shore while carrying heavy fish. They use their wings as oars. While flying, eagles can carry prey about half their weight.

Eagles have rough bumps on their toes that allow them to grasp wriggly fish.

Fish

Squirrels

Rabbits

Raccoons

Rabbits, fish, squirrels, and raccoons are some of the animals eagles eat.

Eagle Life Cycle

Bald eagles have one partner for most of their life. Eagles start laying eggs when they are four to five years old. They lay eggs once a year.

Nesting

The female eagle lays one to three eggs in the spring. Both parents care for the eggs. This includes **incubating** the eggs, hunting for food, and feeding the babies. The eggs hatch in 31 to 45 days.

Chicks

Newly hatched eagle chicks are soft and grayish-white. Their wobbly legs are too weak to hold their weight, and their eyes are partially closed. Their only protection is their parents. The older chicks grab a larger portion of the food.

Eagles make their nest at a height that protects their eggs from harm. They have no natural enemies, other than humans.

Eaglets

At four weeks, chicks are considered to be eaglets. Eaglets are brown in color. A healthy eaglet weighs 9 pounds (4 kg) at six weeks. At this time, they are nearly as large as their parents. By about three months, they are ready for **fledging**.

Adults

At 5 months, eagles are fully grown. By four or five years, their eyes and beak turn yellow. The head and tail feathers change from brown to white. They have a wingspan of 6 to 8 feet (1.8 to 2.4 meters). Eagles can live to be 30 years old in nature. **Captive** eagles can live up to 50 years.

Encountering Eagles

If you have eagles where you live, make sure that your house pets are not out at dawn or dusk. This is the time when eagles hunt, and your pets can be an easy prey.

You may sometimes come face to face with an eagle. The eagle is looking for food and will not attack unless it feels it is in danger from you.

If you happen to be somewhere near an eagle's nest, the mother eagle will make a noise to move you away from her nest. She is very protective about her eggs and babies.

Useful Websites

Check out this site for more interesting information about eagles.
www.eagles.org

One of the world's largest and most powerful eagles is the harpy eagle.

Myths and Legends

An old legend suggests that eagles alone have the power to look into the Sun. The Sun strengthens the eyes of eagles, giving them the gift of sharp vision.

The Aztecs from Mexico respect the eagle as a strong bird. They treasure eagle feathers and often use the feathers to make headwear.

Some American Indian groups have stories about the Thunderbird, a mythical eagle. The mighty Thunderbird created thunder and lightning by clapping its wings. For this reason, eagles were both respected and feared.

A child from the tribe of Mogi Nambka, in Papua New Guinea, wears a headdress made from the feathers of a white eagle.

The Myth of the Clever Eagle

According to an Aboriginal legend, at one time, eagles had very poor eyesight. Still, because they could fly very high, a king asked an eagle to watch for enemies that might harm the kingdom.

Wanting to be of help, the eagle asked a slug for his eyesight,

which was very sharp. The kind slug agreed. Later, the eagle refused to return the slug's eyesight. This is how eagles developed such good vision.

Frequently Asked Questions

How many known species of eagle are there?

Answer: There are 59 species of eagle, found on every continent except Antarctica. The bald eagle and the golden eagle are found in the United States.

How many feathers does an average adult eagle have?

Answer: An adult eagle has about 7,200 feathers, forming half of its body's weight.

How did the bald eagle become the national symbol of the United States?

Answer: The bald eagle was chosen as the national symbol because it is the only type of eagle to be found strictly in North America and nowhere else.

Puzzler

See if you can answer these questions about eagles.

1. Where do eagles build their nests?
2. How long do eagles live?
3. Do eagles have any enemies in nature?
4. Why do eagles migrate?
5. What is the wingspan of adult eagles?

Answers: 1. Tall trees or high cliffs 2. 30 years or more 3. No 4. In search of warm weather and food 5. 6 to 8 feet (1.8 to 2.4 m)

Find Out More

There are many more interesting facts to learn about eagles. Look for these books at your library so you can learn more.

Deborah Hodge. *Eagles*. Kids Can Press, Limited, 2000.

Laura Evert. *Eagles*. T&N Children's Publishing, 2001.

Words to Know

captive: kept in a confined space

carnivores: animals that eat meat

fledging: first flight of an eaglet

fossil: the hardened remains of an animal or plant that lived long ago

habitat: natural living place

incubating: sitting on eggs for the purpose of hatching

migrate: shift from one place to another

talons: long nails on the claws of an eagle

Index